# Nashua Public Library

## Enjoy this book!
Please remember to return it on time
so that others may enjoy it too.

Manage your library account and
discover all we offer by visiting us
online at www.nashualibrary.org

**Love your library? Tell a friend!**

J

SPOTLIGHT ON EXPLORERS AND COLONIZATION™

# SIR FRANCIS DRAKE

## Privateering Sea Captain and Circumnavigator of the Globe

BARBARA KRASNER

**Rosen** PUBLISHING®

New York

Published in 2017 by The Rosen Publishing Group, Inc.
29 East 21st Street, New York, NY 10010

Copyright © 2017 by The Rosen Publishing Group, Inc.

First Edition

**Library of Congress Cataloging-in-Publication Data**

Names: Krasner, Barbara, author.
Title: Sir Francis Drake: Privateering Sea Captain and Circumnavigator of the Globe / Barbara Krasner.
Description: First edition. | New York : Rosen Publishing, 2017. | Series:
  Spotlight on explorers and colonization | Includes bibliographical
  references and index.
Identifiers: LCCN 2016018200 | ISBN 9781508172208 (library bound) | ISBN
  9781508172185 (pbk.) | ISBN 9781508172192 (6-pack)
Subjects: LCSH: Drake, Francis, 1540?–1596—Juvenile literature. | Great
  Britain—History, Naval—Tudors, 1485–1603—Biography—Juvenile literature
  | Great Britain—History—Elizabeth, 1558–1603—Biography—Juvenile
  literature. | Explorers—Great Britain—Biography—Juvenile literature. |
  Admirals—Great Britain—Biography—Juvenile literature.
Classification: LCC DA86.22.D7 K729 2016 | DDC 942.05/5092 [B] —dc23
LC record available at https://lccn.loc.gov/2016018200

*Manufactured in China*

# CONTENTS

# THE AGE OF EXPLORATION

The sixteenth century initiated a period of discovery. Explorers like Ferdinand Magellan of Spain yearned to find a link between the Atlantic and Pacific Oceans. In 1519, he led an expedition of five ships to find and claim that passage for Spain. Despite dangerous obstacles, he successfully navigated to the southern tip of South America, where the two oceans met. It became known as the Strait of Magellan.

England, however, was not to be outdone. Francis Drake wanted to follow in Magellan's footsteps. To do so required Queen Elizabeth's support and her resources. She agreed, but there was a condition: No one

This sixteenth-century portrait of Sir Francis Drake does not fully capture his sense of adventure and loyalty to his queen and country.

must know of Drake's mission. If Spain were to know that the queen permitted raids on Spanish ports, there would surely be war.

Drake knew the definition of danger. He had grown up at sea. He knew how to make the most of very little and how to how to claim bounty for himself.

# DESTINED FOR THE SEAFARING LIFE

**W**hen his family moved from Tavistock to Chatham, a shipbuilding town near London, young Francis Drake was far more interested in sailor stories about lands yet to be discovered than he was in school. His father, Edmund, taught him to read and write. At age twelve, he apprenticed to the owner of a small cargo boat. When the master died, he left the ship to Drake. Now master of his own ship, he spent the next few years using his ship for trade. But he grew bored. He craved adventure. Drake sold his ship and moved to Plymouth, a lively English port.

There the Hawkins family, who were distant relatives, offered him the excitement he wanted. The Hawkinses owned many trading ships. From the Hawkinses he learned the business of piracy, also known as privateering. The English crown encouraged attacks on Spanish ships and claiming treasure for England. Queen Elizabeth even sponsored such voyages.

# THE FIRST VOYAGE TO THE SPANISH MAIN

In 1566, Drake sailed to the Spanish Main, the British name for the Caribbean. Second in command, he learned navigation, and for the first time he fought at sea against Portuguese vessels. He and others seized valuable slaves, sugar, and ivory. The following year, Drake set out again with his relative John Hawkins to the Caribbean. At first he was one of the officers on the expedition's main ship, but he was soon placed in command of a captured Portuguese ship. His ship, the *Gratia Dei* (Grace of God), took part in attacks on Spanish towns. He then became

San Juan de Ulúa in Mexico became a source of embarrassment for Drake. He had not expected defeat and would not stand for it without further action.

captain of a larger ship, the *Judith*. But a raging storm forced Hawkins's ships off course and to the closest port for repair. That port was San Juan de Ulúa, a port for the Spanish fleet along the Gulf of Mexico. The Spaniards crushed Hawkins's ships, except for the *Minion* and the *Judith*. Drake and Hawkins returned home in defeat.

# OUT FOR REVENGE AND TREASURE

By 1571, Francis Drake, now about thirty years old, wanted to fight against the Spanish. He wanted revenge for the defeat at San Juan de Ulúa. But Queen Elizabeth refused to grant him permission to lead a fleet. It would only invite war, and she wanted to avoid that.

Inspired by news he received about French and English pirates' success in raiding Spanish ships, Drake decided to sail anyway. He worked again for the Hawkinses and brothers William and George Wynter. He joined French pirates, and together they conducted a raid up the

On the Isthmus of Panama, Drake became the first Englishman to see the Pacific Ocean, as shown in this late nineteenth-century illustration.

Rio Chagres, cutting through the Isthmus of Panama. On the Pacific Ocean side, he looted forty-seven storerooms at a trading post at Venta de Cruces. He attacked a Spanish frigate near Nombre de Dios. He raided ship after ship, loading up his own with clothing, merchandise, and slaves. Drake returned to England with three ships filled with Spanish booty.

# RAID ON THE TREASURE HOUSE OF THE WORLD

**A**fter a few months of rest, Drake prepared to set sail once again to the Caribbean. He knew now he needed a nimble, or quick and light, ship to navigate the shallow bays, perfect for hiding from the Spanish. He left Plymouth in May 1572, only to encounter mosquitoes and false reports of treasure. Drake vowed to one day sail the Pacific Ocean as he stood overlooking where the two oceans met. In Panama, he and his men carefully staked out treasure trains headed for Nombre de Dios, called the Treasure House of the World. There he

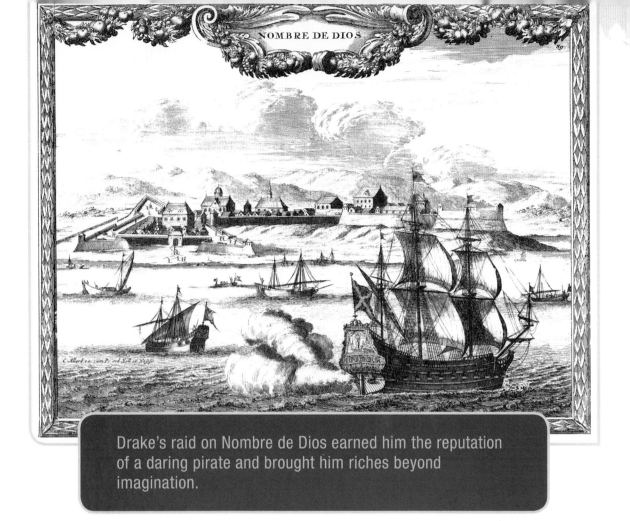

NOMBRE DE DIOS

Drake's raid on Nombre de Dios earned him the reputation of a daring pirate and brought him riches beyond imagination.

launched a successful attack and captured twenty-five tons of silver and gold. Unable to carry that much booty back to England, Drake buried the silver, perhaps giving rise to legends of pirates and buried treasure.

The name "Francis Drake" began to appear in reports of colonial Spanish officials. Cunning and fearless, he was one pirate to watch.

# OFF TO THE AMERICAS, 1577

**I**f a sea route could be found to connect the Far East to Europe directly, that would cut out levies and taxes that led only to overpriced spices and gems. The Spaniards, French, and Portuguese had all made explorations in the New World and established colonies. Why should England not do the same?

Queen Elizabeth remained wary of igniting a war with Spain. But when Drake wrote the government about the readiness of his gun-wielding ship, the *Pelican*, she added a ship, the *Elizabeth*, armed with eleven guns, to his

Ocean voyages presented plenty of risks to pirates and other seafarers. Even Drake's ship, the *Pelican*, as shown here, faced damage.

pursuit. Before he left, the queen presented him with a sea cap, a green silk scarf, and one of her swords.

With the queen's involvement and a promise of great treasure, Drake's five ships set out from Plymouth in November 1577. But a storm quickly damaged the ships, delaying the departure for two weeks.

# THROUGH THE STRAIT OF MAGELLAN

**D**rake set out again with a clear purpose: to reach the Pacific Ocean. But his plan and the queen's support were kept secret until the ships were out at sea. He planned to pass through the Strait of Magellan and sail north along the South American coast to Peru. There he would seize Spanish treasure. The crew was surprised when the ships headed not for the Mediterranean Sea but for Africa. Off the African coast, Drake captured a Portuguese ship but kept the ship's pilot who knew Pacific waters.

Sir Francis Drake gained fame as the explorer who circumnavigated the globe in the name of England. He was away from home for three years.

After two months at sea, the ships caught sight of South America. Drake came up against two problems: the threat of mutiny and a group of gentlemen who did not want to work. He solved this problem by destroying two of his ships. With his crew now aboard the *Pelican*, *Elizabeth*, and *Marigold*, he could better remind them they sailed for the glory of Queen Elizabeth and England.

As Drake reached the Strait of Magellan and the joining of the Atlantic and Pacific Oceans in August 1578, he anchored near three islands. He claimed all three for England. On the largest island, now called Elizabeth Island, Drake conducted a special ceremony. He renamed the *Pelican* as the *Golden Hind.*

They saluted Queen Elizabeth and entered the strait. On its south side, Drake expected to find Tierra del Fuego (land of the fires), so named by Magellan. Mapmakers believed it to be the northernmost tip of a large, unexplored continent, Terra Australis (Australia). It was clear to Drake that Terra Australis lay farther south.

Visitors can board a full-size replica of the *Golden Hind* at Brixham, England and get a sense of what it was like to sail and live on the ship.

In September, after navigating the strait for sixteen days, Drake and his ships finally entered the South Sea. But soon a series of terrifying gales sank the *Marigold*, and the captain of the *Elizabeth* decided to return to England. Only the *Golden Hind* remained.

# DISCOVERY IN SOUTH AMERICA

Crewmembers on sailing vessels in the sixteenth century often suffered from scurvy, a disease caused by a lack of fresh fruits and vegetables. Although the sailors aboard the *Golden Hind* discovered the healing qualities of a certain bark, scurvy might have been the least of their problems. They were not prepared for an attack when they tried to land at an island along the coast of Chile. Although injured himself, Drake refused to fight back with gunfire. The natives had suffered enough at Spanish hands, he reasoned.

The voyage northward along South America's Pacific coast gave Drake the

Ships fighting against each other at sea was inexact. The shifting waters made it difficult to maneuver and carry out attacks.

opportunity to raid Spanish ports and towns. He captured ships and made them his own. However, his growing fleet slowed him down. Most of all, it prevented him from capturing a Spanish ship carrying 500 gold bars and 800 silver bars. Drake decided to let go of all ships but the *Golden Hind.*

# PERUVIAN GOLD

**D**rake learned that Spanish ships in the Callao, Peru, harbor carried vast amounts of silver. But when Drake boarded the ships after their crews went ashore, he discovered no real treasure. He learned another ship had set out for Panama nine days earlier. It carried a large amount of silver for Spain's King Philip II. After Drake offered a gold chain to the crewmember who first sighted the *Cacafuego*, he captured the galleon, and was well rewarded. The ship held 1,300 bars of silver, thirteen chests of silver coins, and eighty pounds of gold.

Drake told the *Cacafuego*'s captain that the queen of England had authorized him to

Caca Fogo.

Caca Plata.

Spanish treasure ships invited Drake's pursuit and attack. He relentlessly went after them for their cargo and to prevent riches from resting in Spanish hands.

make such captures. He knew the captain would report this information in Panama.

Now under pursuit, Drake would have to sail across the Pacific and around the world. Still, that did not stop him from capturing a second ship, full of jewels, gold, and silver.

# CALIFORNIA!

**D**rake sailed along the coast of Central and North America. As far north as he sailed, farther than any other European, he looked for but did not find a northwest passage connecting the Atlantic and Pacific Oceans. He set anchor in a large bay along the California coast. He claimed the land for England and named it Nova Albion (New Britain), now thought to be Marin County, in 1579. Drake was planning for England's future colonization of these islands. He and his crew went ashore and stayed five weeks using the time to repair the ship and replenish supplies. They explored the

**V.**

## FRANCISCVS DRACO CVM
### IN LOCVM QVENDAM VENIS-
set, à Rege istius regionis conuenitur.

*Vm Franciscus Draco aliquando ad locum quendam in America veniset, vidit in litto-re quædam incolarum tuguria, quæ ex rotundis paludibus vel arboribus potius compacta, & in formam pyramidis fastigiata, ab externa parte terra vndique oppleta erant. Cumq, ea ingressus esset, inuenit homines in circumferentia, confuse in stramine dormientes, nullo vel ætatis vel sexus seruato discrimine, qui in medio domus ingentem ignem extruxerant. Hi homines Anglis multa exhibebant beneficia, cumq, de eorum aduentu Rex audiuisset, venit eò cum 12000 viris, satis splendide magnificeq. Ac omnes quidem sub-diti sui nudi incedebant, ipse vero solus cuniculorum pellibus vestitus erat. Eum caduceator præcedebat, sce-ptrum & regalia regni gestans. Hunc cum DRACO vidsset, instructa statim acie, aduentum eius expecta-uit, sed ipse pacifice veniens, prolixa eum oratione per caduceatorem allocutus est, finitaque oratione imposuit ei duas coronas de sceptro siue caduceo dependentes, & tres catenulas ex ossibus artificiose factas à collo eius su-spendit, quibus ipsi se & totum suum regnum imperiumq, subiicere voluit. Interea mulieres etiam non paucæ accedebant, quæ præ lætitia, maxillas & faciem, ad sanguinem vsque lacerârant, incedebant ipsæ quoque nudæ, nisi quod femorali ex scirpis facto, pudenda aliquo modo circumdederant, & ab humeris pellem ceruinam de-pendentem habebant.*

b 2

land and befriended the local Miwoks in their villages and huts. The Miwoks crowned him in a special ceremony.

The most dangerous journey lay ahead of him: crossing the vast Pacific Ocean. To help him navigate, he would need to rely on maps taken from a captured Spanish ship.

# ROUNDING THE CAPE OF GOOD HOPE

The *Golden Hind* spent more than two months heading toward the Moluccas, also known as the Spice Islands. Spices were coveted and some, such as pepper, nutmeg, cinnamon, and cloves, were worth their weight in gold in Europe. They enhanced the flavor of food and were used for perfumes and medicines. The spice trade had made Portugal as rich as the New World's silver and gold had made Spain rich. Finally, the crew spotted land, and the ship maneuvered through the chain of some 1,600 islands of the Philippines.

When Drake arrived in the Spice Islands, he found a state of unrest. The sultan

Nutmeg could be found on a certain tree in the Spice Islands, now part of Indonesia. The Dutch came to control the spice in the century following Drake's agreement.

wanted to be free of Portuguese rule. Drake made an agreement with the sultan that in exchange for helping him gain freedom, England would receive exclusive rights to the spices.

The *Golden Hind* rounded the Cape of Good Hope, and Drake set his course for home.

# A THANKFUL QUEEN

**A** year later, in September 1580, Drake and the *Golden Hind* arrived in Plymouth once more. The ship was loaded with treasure. The first Englishman to circumnavigate the world, Drake became the most famous man in Europe.

Queen Elizabeth honored him as a hero. She named him to a new Royal Commission on the Navy. She claimed half his cargo. If war with Spain was coming, Drake's treasure would prove most useful. Elizabeth gave instructions that a rumor be started that he had returned with little treasure. She wrote Drake to bring her specimens of his finds. He loaded horses with gold and silver and with an armed escort headed to

This replica of the *Golden Hind* makes it easy to imagine Drake's return to his home port of Plymouth, England.

London. He distributed treasure to himself and the crew. The rest was taken to the Tower of London and locked up.

Meanwhile, the Spanish ambassador watched Drake carefully. He reported Drake's spending and time with Queen Elizabeth to King Philip.

# A POLICY OF SECRETS

**W**ith Spanish eyes watching, Queen Elizabeth had to be cautious. She declared all written accounts of Drake's voyages as secrets of her realm. That included an account written by the chaplain aboard the *Golden Hind,* titled *The World Encompassed by Sir Francis Drake*. All maps had to be concealed.

That the queen favored Drake was obvious to members of the royal court. She called upon him to accompany her on her daily walks. But some people in the court wondered whether he was really just a master thief.

Secrets ended with the queen's April 1581 visit to the *Golden Hind*, where she knighted

Knighthood is a way for Britain's royalty to honor and reward people. Here Queen Elizabeth I taps a sword on Drake's shoulders to bestow knighthood on him.

him. Books, portraits, and pamphlets using his likeness emerged. Through his knighthood and additional purchases, Sir Francis Drake became the second largest private landowner in Plymouth with twenty-nine houses. As a knight, it was only natural that he become mayor of Plymouth and a member of Parliament's House of Commons.

# THE DRAGON AND HIS RETURN TO THE WEST INDIES

In May 1585, news reached London that King Philip II of Spain had captured many English trading ships in Spanish and Portuguese ports. By September, to retaliate against Spain's aggression, Drake assembled some twenty ships with Queen Elizabeth's permission. The Dragon, as the Spaniards called Drake, was out for revenge and to capture more of Spain's wealth in the New World.

This 1589 map illustrates a section of Drake's West Indian voyage. Here Drake's fleet is anchored at Santiago, off the coast of Africa, in 1585.

But unlike previous expeditions, more than a thousand soldiers sailed with Drake. There was a list of towns to attack: Santo Domingo, the most important Spanish stronghold in the New World, Cartagena, Panama, and Havana.

The English wanted to replace the Spaniards and take control of these towns.

The venture began with a raid on the port of Vigo in northern Spain. Drake captured and plundered ships. The next port of call was the Cape Verde Islands and its town of Santiago. There a deadly fever claimed nearly 300 of Drake's men.

Once he reached the Caribbean, he attacked Santo Domingo in Hispaniola and raided it for riches, especially in the churches. He also led a surprise raid on Cartagena. His men continued to die from the fever, however, and the expedition was not achieving its goals. Drake and his captains decided to bypass Panama and head for Cuba. But they did not stop there either. Whether planned or unplanned, Drake sailed along the coast of North America and destroyed the Spanish fort of St. Augustine in Florida.

As he moved up the coast, he and his men stopped at the English settlement at Roanoke off the coast of the Carolinas. The

Though this map from 1600 does not resemble a map of the Florida we know today, it does show Drake's ships at the Spanish settlement of St. Augustine in 1586.

colonists were ill equipped to survive there. They were running out of supplies and wanted to go home. Drake brought them back to England. He reached the British port of Portsmouth in July 1586.

# THE ULTIMATE BATTLE: DRAKE AGAINST THE SPANISH ARMADA

**K**ing Philip wanted to stop Drake once and for all—and control England. He built up a fleet of warships, better known as the Armada, and initiated his "Enterprise of England" attack.

Drake was able to convince Queen Elizabeth to give him a new commission, so he set out with twenty-four ships and 3,000 men. His first encounter against the Armada took place at Cadiz. He only managed to destroy a small portion of the Armada.

A seventeenth-century Spanish painter captured the scene of Drake's raid at Cardiz in 1587. Drake occupied the harbor for three days.

The Spanish were ready for him at Lagos, and Drake was forced to retreat. He headed to the Portuguese capital of Lisbon, where the Armada was assembling. But rather than attacking it, he blocked sea traffic to delay the king's plans.

Philip launched his Armada of 130 ships and 15,000 troops on May 20, 1588. Instead of a triumphant victory, however, bad weather damaged the ships and repairs took another month.

Drake's defeat of the mighty Spanish Armada has become legend. Nearly 300 years after the battle, an artist created this illustration of the dramatic event.

Under the British class system, even a naval hero like Drake could not become high commander of the navy. Queen Elizabeth gave overall command of the British navy to Lord Howard of Effingham. He was an experienced sailor, and as her chamberlain, the queen could trust him. Drake was named second in command.

The English fleet included both royal and private ships. Drake commanded the *Revenge*, a royal ship. Over the years, Drake had become a master of military strategy and could use weather conditions to his advantage. Still, when the British fleet tried three times to meet the Armada, it, too, faced bad weather and fierce winds. It waited for battle in the English Channel.

By mid-July, the Armada had reached the southwest edge of England. The British fleet relentlessly pursued the Spanish ships. Its small, well-armed ships could out-maneuver Spain's large warships. By early August, the remains of the mighty Armada limped home, and Drake became more popular than ever.

# FROM PRIVATEER TO LEGENDARY EXPLORER

The defeat of the Armada did not dampen Drake's desire to be at sea. He was selected to lead a campaign to end the Armada forever. But this campaign against Spanish-controlled Portugal was too much for him physically and mentally, and it failed.

His attempts to raid Spanish towns failed, too. So much had changed since his first ventures to the Spanish Main. These towns no longer offered adventure or profit. Sickness invaded his ships. He contracted dysentery and died. He was buried at sea near Panama in January 1596.

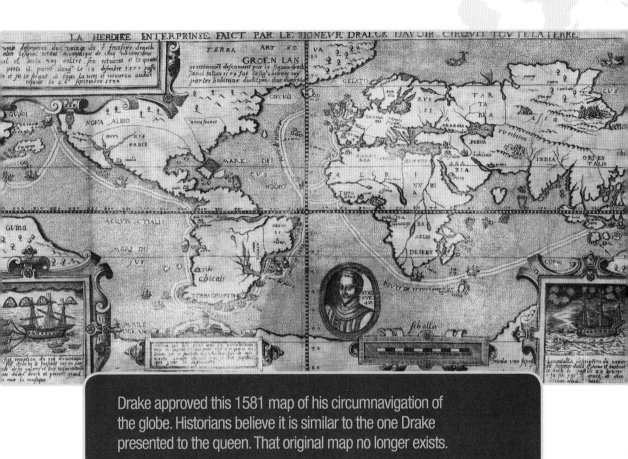

Drake approved this 1581 map of his circumnavigation of the globe. Historians believe it is similar to the one Drake presented to the queen. That original map no longer exists.

Drake's "secret" voyage and his circumnavigation marked the turning point of his career, when he shed the label of rogue and earned the reputation of legendary explorer. The defeat of the Armada turned him into a respected naval leader. While historians continue to debate his true contributions, they agree that Sir Francis Drake was at his best while at sea.

# GLOSSARY

**booty**  The spoils of a raid or war, taken from an enemy.

**bounty**  The reward gained from a raid.

**chamberlain**  An officer who manages the king's or queen's household.

**circumnavigate**  To sail around the world.

**dysentery**  An infectious stomach disease.

**frigate**  A medium-sized ship that became popular in the eighteenth and nineteenth centuries.

**galleon**  A large sailing ship.

**Hispaniola**  An island in the West Indies, now called Haiti and the Dominican Republic.

**isthmus**  A narrow strip of land surrounded by water on both sides that connects two bodies of land.

**levies**  Taxes, fees, or fines.

**maneuver**  To move a ship through obstacles.

**Miwoks**  A Native American people previously living north of San Francisco, California.

**mutiny**  A ship crew's revolt against its commander.

**Parliament**  An assembly of nobles and representatives that helps England's rulers.

**plunder**  To take goods or valuables by force.

**port of call**  A port town or city that a ship visits.

**scurvy**  A deadly disease caused by a lack of vitamin C that affected sailors on long voyages.

**strait**  A narrow passage that connects two large bodies of water.

**sultan**  A ruler who reigns with absolute power.

**vessel**  A ship or boat that travels on water.

The British Museum
Great Russell Street
London WC1B 3DG
United Kingdom
Website: http://www.britishmuseum.org
The British Museum houses some artifacts of Sir
    Francis Drake.

The Explorers Club
46 East 70th Street
New York, NY 10021
(212) 628-8383
Website: https://explorers.org
The Explorers Club is a professional organization of
    explorers and scientists interested in land, sea, air,
    and space.

MIT Institute
Archives and Special Collections
Cambridge Building
Cambridge, MA 02142
(617) 253-5136
Website: https://libraries.mit.edu/archives/exhibits/
    drake
MIT Archives holds a report about a brass plaque
    claimed to be written by Sir Francis Drake in 1579.

Royal Museums Greenwich
National Maritime Museum
Greenwich, London SE10 9NF
United Kingdom
Website: http://www.rmg.co.uk
The National Maritime Museum is part of Royal
    Museums Greenwich. The museum has paintings
    of Sir Francis Drake.

St. Augustine Art Association
22 Marine Street
St. Augustine, FL 32084
(904) 824-2310
Website: http://www.staaa.org
A special exhibit at this association's location shows
    artifacts from Drake's raid on St. Augustine in 1586.

# Websites

Because of the changing nature of internet links, Rosen
Publishing has developed an online list of websites
related to the subject of this book. This site is updated
regularly. Please use this link to access the list:

http://www.rosenlinks.com/SEC/drake

Anderson, Michael. *Biographies of the New World* (Impact on America). New York, NY: Britannica Educational Publishing, 2013.

Clements, Gillian. *The Spanish Armada.* London, UK: Franklin Watts, 2014.

Croce, Pat. *Sir Francis Drake.* St. Augustine, FL: Pirate & Maritime Research Society, 2013.

Davidson, Susanna. *Queen Elizabeth I.* London, UK: Usborne, 2014.

Gould, Jane. *Ferdinand Magellan* (Jr. Graphic Famous Explorers). New York, NY: PowerKids Press, 2013.

Krull, Kathleen. *Lives of the Pirates: Swashbucklers, Scoundrels* (Neighbors Beware!). Boston, MA: Houghton Mifflin Harcourt/Sandpiper, 2013.

Nardo, Don. *Sir Francis Drake* (Pirates Around the World: Terror on the High Seas). Hockessin, DE: Mitchell Lane, 2015.

Pletcher, Kenneth. *The Britannica Guide to Explorers and Adventurers.* New York, NY: Britannica Educational Publishing, 2013.

Sheehan, Robert. *Francis Drake: Patriot or Pirate?* (Discovery Education: Sensational True Stories). New York, NY: PowerKids Press, 2013.

Vaux, William Sandys Wright. *The World Encompassed by Sir Francis Drake.* Farnham Surrey, UK: Ashgate Publishing Group, 2010.

Wood, Alix. *Pirates on the Map* (Fun with Map Skills). New York, NY: PowerKids Press, 2014.

# BIBLIOGRAPHY

Bawlf, Samuel. *The Secret Voyage of Sir Francis Drake, 1577–1580.* New York NY: Walker & Co., 2003.

Frear Keeler, Mary. *Sir Francis Drake's West Indian Voyage, 1585–86.* Farnham, UK: Hakluyt Society, 2011.

Kelsey, Harry. *Sir Francis Drake: The Queen's Pirate.* New Haven, CT: Yale University Press, 1998.

Sugden, John. *Sir Francis Drake.* New York, NY: Henry Holt, 1990.

Thrower, Norman J. W., ed. *Sir Francis Drake and the Famous Voyage, 1577–1580: Essays Commemorating the Quadricentennial of Drake's Circumnavigation of the Earth.* Berkeley, CA: University of California Press, 1984.

Vaux, William Sandys Wright. *The World Encompassed by Sir Francis Drake.* Farnham Surrey, UK: Ashgate Publishing Group, 2010.

Whitfield, Peter. *Sir Francis Drake.* New York, NY: New York University Press, 2004.

Wilson, Derek. T*he World Encompassed: Drake's Great Voyage, 1577–1580.* New York, NY: Harper & Row, 1977.

# About the Author

Barbara Krasner is a historian and author of more than twenty books. She holds a master's degree in history and a master's degree in writing for children and young adults. Pirates and anything Elizabethan fascinate her. She lives in New Jersey.

# Photo Credits